Crowdfunding With Kickstarter:
A Beginner's Guide To Crowdfunding Success

Vincent Gallo

NMD Books
Simi Valley, CA

Library of Congress Cataloging-in-Publication

Crowdfunding With Kickstarter: A Beginner's Guide To Crowdfunding Success By Vincent Gallo

ISBN: 978-1-936828-36-4

First Edition January 2015

Contents

How to Use This Guide

Read it, study it, memorize it and then IGNORE IT.

This e-book is a not a step by step manual on how to get your project funded. I don't think there is any formula that can guarantee success. Instead, it is a collection of thoughts and ideas to help you create the best Kickstarter campaign possible. If the ideas in this book don't fit your project or don't resonate with you, then try something else.

At the end, of the day remember one thing: There is no map. to successfully fund your creative project.

Why am I Writing This?

The first time I heard about Kickstarter.com, I loved the idea. As a person who always has creative ideas, I understood the value of being able to test the market for an idea while building an audience. So many amazing and wonderful ideas never had a viable way to launch, until now.

Even though Kickstarter is a great platform for creative types such as myself, it's not enough to simply post a project on the site and expect the Internet to do the rest. Not everyone will love our ideas, but there is a lot we can do to help the idea spread. I firmly, believe the better we are at communicating and marketing our ideas, the more successful we will ultimately be.

Introduction

"The mindset is, how can I find more customers for my products? ... Maybe, you should start thinking bout, how do I find more products for my customers?"
- Seth Godin

We often hear stories of someone posting a creative project online. Then hundreds or thousands of people come rushing to them and it takes off. It seems so simple. Come up with a brilliant idea and the Internet will take over to make our dreams come true.

Somewhere deep down inside we know there is more to it than that. There must be some explanation as to why their idea took off. We're just not sure what it is. We launch our own project, hoping the masses will show up, but they never do. We are left feeling disappointed and full of doubt. Why not me? Was my idea not good enough?

The truth is that there is a lot of work that goes into a project before it will take off. Simply posting an idea online is rarely enough to get meaningful traction. That's the lesson I learned, the hard way.

In the fall of 2010 I posted my first Kickstarter project. It was for a documentary film that I wanted to make with a friend of mine. After our project got approved we naively rushed through setting up the project page and launched it. Confident in the fact that we had the best looking video on the site with a meaningful topic, we sat back and waited.

After a month we had only raised 10% of our goal. Slightly disheartened and running out of time, we rolled up our sleeves and began contacting everyone we knew. In three weeks we were able to raise an additional $5000. However, there was only one week to go, and we had over 50% of our funding goal left.

Faced with the reality that our project probably would not make it, I started to question myself and my idea. Then something amazing happened. Realizing the deadline was fast approaching, my friends started posting it, writing emails and sharing it with their friends. In the last six days we raised $9000 and got the project successfully funded!

If this sounds like another example of a viral Internet phenomena, I assure it's not.

My project never got picked up by any major media or high profile blogs. In fact, the

ONLY reason that my campaign succeeded is because I have amazing friends and family who rallied to support me. Even with all their support, we limped to the finish line. I feel pretty lucky that we made it at all. But I'm ok with being lucky.

In the months after the Kickstarter campaign ended, I was able to reflect on my campaign. I thought about everything I could have done differently that could have made it even better. I started to looked at what other people did to fund their projects.

I began to realize that it was not my idea that had been the problem, but my approach. I had made a lot of assumptions about how the idea would be spread and how Kickstarter worked. From those insights this guide was born.

In the world of Kickstarter there is a lot that happens behind the scenes to make a project successful. Just because an idea is great or worth doing doesn't mean it's going to get funded. Rather than trying to guess at what those factors are, this manifesto will look at what it takes to make a project successful.

In case you don't have time to read this in entirety, this is what it says in a nutshell:

Great Kickstarter projects are successful because they connect and resonate with a specific audience. They use compelling storytelling combined with interesting or wacky ideas to attract backers. They are authentic while effectively communicating goals, passion, credibility and purpose. The more time spent thinking about these elements BEFORE the project is launched the easier the campaign becomes.

If you want to do a Kickstarter project because you think the Internet will find and love your project, stop right now. The Internet does not care about you. However, if you can reach out to the right people, in the right way, before time runs out, you just might get lucky.

Understanding Kickstarter

From Humble Beginings

Kickstarter was founded in 2009 by Perry Chen, Yancey Strickler, and Charles Adler. Since its launch over 10,000 projects have been successfully funded, with people pledging more than 75 million dollars. However, Kickstarter wasn't always this big. Much like your project, Kickstarter began small.

In 2002 Perry was working in New Orleans and trying to put together a concert. He wanted a way to query the audience to see if he had enough support to go through with it. From this initial idea Kickstarter.com was born. However, it would take another seven years before the site would launch.

"I didn't necessarily know where to begin. I wasn't coming from working on the web" says Perry in an interview with TechCrunch. "At the time...I couldn't have been less interested in dedicating my life, which is clearly what it takes." Fortunately for us, he met some like-minded individuals and began working on the site.

A couple years, later Perry moved back to New York City, his hometown. He met Yancey while working as a waiter at a restaurant called Diner in Brooklyn. Yancey was a regular and worked as a journalist. One day Perry mentioned an idea he had for a site that would allow him to raise money for creative projects. Yancey liked the idea and they began working it. However, neither of them had technical backgrounds. It wasn't until they met Charles Adler that the idea really started to take off.

Recalling the early years, Yancey said "At the beginning... it was a few people with a piece of paper and not much else." He spoke of how they would wake up every morning wondering "Is today the day that the three people who live in Palo Alto, who are working on the exact same idea launch their site?"

In order to get the site funded they reached out to David Cross, an actor on Arrested

Development. Perry was friends with David's cousin, and she helped arrange the meeting. David came on as the initial investor and was joined by a few other artists later. When they were finally ready to launch, they sent invitations out to 30 of their friends and asked them to share it with five of their friends. In essence, they kick started their own site.

The Basics

Kickstarter is a platform for someone with a creative project to obtain financing for their idea by receiving small amounts of money from a larger group of people. Each project has a public page, funding amount, deadline and rewards.

The funding goal is the minimum amount of money that a project needs in order to happen. If a funding goal is not met by the deadline, the people backing the project are not charged, and the creator receives no money. This may seem a bit harsh, but it is a very important aspect to the way Kickstarter works.

Deadlines are set by the project creator and can be as long as 60 days. According to the Kickstarter School shorter projects tend to be more successful than longer projects. The number of days remaining in a campaign is displayed on each project page.

The project page provides all the information about the project. This usually includes a written description, video and rewards. I will go in detail about each of these aspects later.

Rewards are an important part of Kickstarter, and each project is required to offer them. Rewards come in many forms, from a physical product, to services, to early access. They depend on how much someone pledges to support a project.

During the campaign a creator can post updates about how the project is going. These updates can be for the general public or just for the people who have already backed the project. Once the project is completed, the creator is responsible for honoring the rewards that were offered during the campaign.

The Patron Model

In tech circles raising small amounts of money from a large group of people is commonly called "crowdfunding" or "crowd-sourced funding." This is a buzz word and does not actually describe what happens on Kickstarter. Who is this crowd? Where do they come from? How do they find us? The word crowdfunding makes it seem so easy.

All we have to do is post a project and the crowd will fund it. However, that's not really what happens.

Founder Perry Chen describes Kickstarter as a newer version of the patron model, which lies somewhere between altruism and capitalism. People not only give to a project because they like the idea or creator, but they also get something in return. The reward could be to see the project come into existence or to get one of the Kickstarter rewards created for the site.

The idea has been around for a very long time. Mozart and Beethoven used a similar funding model to premiere concerts and first print editions of their works. Patrons of the visual arts were rewarded by being able to keep and display the artwork. The Kickstarter model is similar, but it's turbocharged by the web and its social aspects.

The web allows for ideas to spread very fast and helps connect creators with an audience. The all or nothing deadline encourages patrons to share and promote the project quickly or risk see it disappear. Fueled by Facebook, Twitter and other social sites, Kickstarter projects can take on a life of their own, as patrons spread the idea far and wide.

Girl Scout Cookies

On the final day of my Kickstarter campaign for A Kickstarter's Guide I got this wonderful tweet.

@Danielle_VBF
DanielleVonFulenberg

@dewittn @Kickstarter is like investing in your friend's kids Girl Scout cookies without the calories

5 Sep via HootSuite ☆ Favorite ↻ Retweet ↩ Reply

Danielle might have been joking but I think she is on to something. Kickstarter is very much like purchasing girl scout cookies. Not only are you helping the girl scouts, but you are getting some great cookies. It's not exactly charity and its not exactly capitalism. Kickstarter lies somewhere in between. People support you and your project but also get something concrete in return.

A Sea of Projects

"Projects. Projects. Projects. Kickstarter is for the funding of projects – albums, films, specific works – that have clearly defined goals and expectations."
- Kickstarter.com guide lines.

Why is Kickstarter so obsessed with projects? Because they are tangible and help focus creators and their audience. Projects have specific goals, deadlines, and outcomes. This makes it easy for potential backers to understand where their money is going. Ideas without specific objectives are harder to support because the outcome is unknown. Projects also work well with Kickstarter's all or nothing model, because patrons have an easy way to tell which projects are definitely going to happen.

A Creative Edge

Kickstarter describes itself as "a new way to fund & follow creativity." It is geared toward, and is an important site for the creative arts.

Perry Chen explains:

"The landscape for creative ideas has been really constrained, because ideas need to be revenue generating... so most ideas are thrown away. What we are hoping is that other 99% of ideas can now come to a place like Kickstarter and get community funded."

"By not forcing things to have to generate revenue, you give them a chance to really come to life... [In the past] those [projects] have been supported by grants, rich uncles, and foundations."

Kickstarter provides a space for these creative ideas to be funded.

In order to post a project on the site it must be within the parameters Kickstarter establishes.

> **"Kickstarter can be used to fund projects from the creative fields of Art, Comics, Dance, Design, Fashion, Film, Food, Games, Music, Photography, Publishing, Technology, and Theater. We currently only support projects from these categories."**
> *- Kickstarter.com guidelines.*

What if your project is not in the "creative arts?" Don't get discouraged, for Kickstarter uses the term liberally. Many projects that you may not think would be classified as "creative arts" get accepted by Kickstarter. However, all projects must have some creative element in them. If you are considering using Kickstarter.com to raise funds, make sure you read through the guidelines in its entirety.

All Shapes and Sizes

With over 10,000 successful campaigns, there are a wide variety of Kickstarter projects. However, most are trying to do one of the following.

Kickstart a Larger Project

Kickstarter is a great way to fund parts of larger projects or businesses. I used the site to start Identifying Nelson. Others have used it as a way to launch a product which turned into a business.

Finish a Project

Zach and Jonathan used Kickstarter to save Blue Like Jazz (the movie) and raise money to complete the film. They are not the only movie that used Kickstarter to help put the finishing touches on their project.

Pre-sale

One of the most famous Kickstarter projects, TikTok+LunaTik Multi-Touch Watch Kits, used Kickstarter as a way to pre-sell their kits. It's a great way to test the market for a product before actually committing to making it. If the product doesn't sell, you haven't put any of your own money on the table.

Support a Community

The team behind Diaspora used Kickstarter to create an open-source Facebook alternative. Since the final product was free to download once they were done, you did not necessarily have to support the campaign on Kickstarter. However, by supporting the project, the whole open-source community benefited.

Spread an Idea

Because of the viral potential of Kickstarter, it is great for spreading ideas. If your project really resonates with an audience, it might spread far and wide. The Manual, a project about improving design principles, used the site to publish a book and spread the idea of better design to a larger community.

Do Something Fun

Ever wanted to build a giant Robocop statue in downtown Detroit? That's exactly what the Imagination Station Detroit team did. They used Kickstarter as a way to get a life-sized Robocop statue built the heart of Detroit. They even got the actor who played Robocop on board. How cool is that?

The Process

Each step has its own unique set of challenges.

Proposal

This is a written description of your project that will be evaluated by Kickstarter, to see if it fits within the requirements for the site.

Consists of a title, category, funding goal, 1500 character description of the project and a 1000 character description of the rewards.

Project Page

What people will see when they click your project. It displays the amount you are going for, how much time there is left until the project finishes its run, rewards, a written description and a video. While a project is not required to have a video, Kickstarter highly recommends it.

Launch

This is when things heat up. Once your project is launched it's you against the clock. It's a race against time to get the word out about your project and let everyone know what you are up to. During this phase you spend most of your time contacting people.

Ending

Assuming your campaign has been successful, it's time to get to the fun part, remembering you will be responsible for fulfilling rewards and keeping your backers updated about your progress.

The Benefits

It is a great way to build support for a project that you want to do. It also has additional benefits such as:

Connecting to an audience - This can be an existing audience or one that you build through the campaign. You will be able to ask them for support, exchange ideas, make friends, and do business. Having a group of people that you can turn to repeatedly, will make launching future endeavors that much easier.

Cutting out the middleman - In many industries such as film and music, one must go through a middleman in order to have a project funded. With Kickstarter the fans are the people who fund your project. If they want to support you and see it happen, then it will.

Exchanging value - That means that both the project creator and the backer get something from the transaction. The project creator gets to see his or her idea come to life, and backers get a reward. This could be a cool new product or the good feeling from helping a friend.

Retaining control - Traditionally, when working with middlemen and other organizations, they end up owning the rights to your artistic work. On Kickstarter this is not the case.

You retain full control and are free to do whatever you would like with the finished product.

Gaining Permission - When people back your project, they are not only giving you money, but they're giving you permission to talk to them about your ideas and future projects. Every time you send a message to your backers it goes right into their inbox. Like many other forms of digital marketing, you now have a way to talk directly to people who want to hear from you.

Getting funded

So what does it take to get funded? That is a key question, the one I'll be exploring in this book. For now, I thought I would share some of the founders' thoughts on what they think it takes to get funded.

Each Project is a Story

During a talk co-founder Yancey Strickler gave earlier this year, he explains how every project is the story.

> **"Each Kickstarter project is a narrative of a real person doing something important or something meaningful, something they care about. We get to follow along. We get to act as an audience. These are people talking to their audience's peers. These are people just like you and I, trying to raise money for an idea, trying to build support for their idea from people just like you and I."**
> **- Yancey Strickler, Creative Mornings June 2011**

Strickler goes on to explain that Kickstarter is a video-driven site. When people come to a project page, the first thing they do is click on the video to see what the project is all about. He calls the videos "anti-commercials" because they are like advertisements for an idea, but authentic.

The other way that stories are told are through rewards. Great rewards tell the story and share the experience with the audience.

Yancey on Why projects fail

Yancey Stickler believes projects that fail, do so for several reasons. Either the creator is going for too much money, or he or she has no history or "proof of concept."

Creators either have unrealistic expectations, or they are too commercial.

Perry's Six Principles

In 2009, only five weeks after Kickstarter launched, Perry Chen gave an Ignite talk about what makes a successful project. Even though the site was still very young, many of the ideas he presented still hold true.

1) Be Real - "It's humans asking other humans to help them."

2) Have a clear goal - "It's not sponsor my life. It's not fund me as an artist for some vague pursuit."

3) Offer fun rewards - "It's about finding ways to provide value to the people who are helping you out."

4) Show you can execute - "So anyone can throw up a page, anyone can have idea, but before people are going to open their wallets they want to know you can execute."

5) Involve the audience - "The line between creators and the audience is getting blurred every day."

6) Spread the word - "Your idea isn't going to mutate out there. Your going to need to push it out there and get your friends to help you spread the word."

"If you do these six things, you are going to have a really great crowd-funding experience."
- Perry Chen

Brainstorming Your Project

Thinking it Through

Now that you have a basic understanding of how Kickstarter works, it's time to focus on getting your project together. During this phase you will start to refine your project, think about how long it will run, your funding amount, and some things you can offer as rewards. You probably have an idea for something you want to try on Kickstarter and a general sense of how much you will go for. Before you move on to the next phase you will want to be very clear about your idea and project.

"What is This Damn Thing About?"

In *Do the Work,* Steven Pressfield talks about the challenges of taking on creative endeavors. He says we often get off track because our ideas aren't refined enough. One way around this is to constantly ask yourself: "What is this damn thing about?"

This is a great place to start with your Kickstarter project. Can you clearly state what your project is about and what the outcome will be? The most successful projects on

Kickstarter can. If you are having trouble, then your idea or project might not be ready for launch. That's OK. You don't need to rush it. I wish I had taken more time to think things through during my first project. It would have made everything much easier.

One great way to get feedback about your idea is to tell some friends. Friends are great because they're honest sounding boards. If they can't understand what you are trying to do, then how is a stranger going to? Ask them what they like and dislike about your idea. You don't have to follow their advice, but you should at least listen.

Often projects are unclear because they are too big and complicated. Next you will need to figure out what the outcome of your project will be. This is going help you refine your idea and get the project into a form that works well on Kickstarter.

Simplify

Kickstarter works best with projects that have clear outcomes and specific goals.

Larger projects with multiple parts are harder to get funded. I will get into the logistics of this a little later. For now, spend time thinking about what the specific outcome of your project is going to be. Your project does not have to be simple, but the outcome should be. Here are some examples of specific outcomes:

- Writing an e-book
- Making an album
- Finishing post-production on a film
- Making a pen

Films and other large projects have many different parts to them. If your project is similar, try to break it down into smaller parts, such as filming, editing, post-production, etc. Each part should have a specific goal and outcome. Projects that are too general may not get approved by Kickstarter and, as stated earlier, are more difficult to get funded.

A project to "start a pen business" will not be approved by Kickstarter. It is too broad and does not have a clear outcome. Even if it was approved, it would be hard to get funded. Potential backers want to know exactly what your project is about. If it is not clear, they may hesitate to spend money on your project. Instead, focus on a smaller slice of the business like launching your first line of ballpoints.

Purple Cows

Once you come up with some specific goals and outcomes, start thinking about all the creative things you can do with your project. You want to make the idea of what you are doing as interesting as possible. Remarkable ideas have a much easier time getting funded. Spend some time to think about how you can make your project as wacky, zany and fun as possible.

There are so many people that want to make films, albums, books, games, etc. that you need to do something to make your idea stand out. But what makes an idea remarkable? It depends on the people who are going to like your project. If they think it's cool, then they will talk about it. I will talk more about audience in the next section. For now, just think about all the different ways you could spice up your project.

I won't pretend to be a master at creating remarkable ideas. I'm still learning myself. If you really need help making your idea cool, check out Seth Godin's book Purple Cow. It's all about how to make your product, idea or business remarkable. I've read it several times and each time I learn something new.

A great example of a "purple cow" was a project to build a statue of Robocop in downtown Detroit. The idea was so remarkable that it got featured on high profile blogs and was overfunded by $17,000. The project was very successful even though the project video was nothing more than a ten-minute recap of the movie. Remarkable ideas spread on their own and don't need a lot of help to catch people's attention.

Detroit Needs A Statue of Robocop! by Imagination Station Detroit — Kickstarter

Making an idea creative and interesting is very hard and you may not get it right the first time. I know I didn't. Just keep working at it and getting feedback from friends. When people start to say "Hey that's a neat idea!" then you might be on to something.

Making Lemonade

After you have added some fun to your project, think about how you are going to tell your story. A powerful tool, that lies at the heart of Kickstarter, is storytelling. Sometimes the way you talk about your project is more important than the product itself. Being able to tell a compelling story is very hard. When done right, it can move people.

In 2009 I came across one of my favorite YouTube videos of all time. It was a trailer for a movie called Lemonade. The movie was about advertising professionals that have been laid off and were starting over. What I love about the Lemonade trailer is that in 2:17 the narrator tells a complete story in a meaningful way. You connect with the people and the subject matter. Even if you have never been laid off, you can feel their pain and bitterness.

When telling your story on Kickstarter you should strive for a similar effect. If people can connect emotionally with your project, they will be more likely to back it or share it. The story that you tell on Kickstarter does not need to be as well produced as the Lemonade trailer.

However, the more thought you put into how you will tell the story the more impact it will have.

The Lockpicks project by Schuyler Towne is probably one of my favorite examples of storytelling. I found it while building the campaign for Identifying Nelson. He tells the story so well that it draws in people who do not share his passion. I'm not interested in lock-picking, but by the end of this video, I am! I want one. I don't even know what I would do with with a kit, but the story he tells makes it seem so exciting!

*Lockpicks by Open Locksport by Schuyler Towne —
Kickstarter*

Reward the patrons

At this point in the process you probably have some ideas for rewards. Some rewards are obvious. For example, if you're making a book, then a possible reward is a print copy of the book. Other rewards might not be as easy to come up with.

Really think about all the different things you can do and offer as rewards. Just like your main idea, you want them to be as creative as possible. Rewards are an important part of Kickstarter because they are where the most "value" is exchanged. Having compelling and fun rewards are all part of the Kickstarter experience.

One thing to think about is the difference between physical goods and digital goods. Digital goods are easy to replicate and cost very little. Physical goods cost more to produce but have a higher intrinsic value. It's not that digital goods are meaningless. In fact, they can be quite valuable. However, they don't invoke the same feeling as physical goods. Think about receiving a handwritten letter vs. the hundreds of emails we get every day. There is a reason why wedding invitations are still sent via "snail mail." Treat your physical awards as souvenirs, and give them to people who care the most about your project.

Don't worry about pricing your rewards just yet; that will come later. For now, generate a list that you can come back to later. As the details of your project become clearer, you will have a better sense of which rewards will work best for your project.

Types of Rewards

There are rewards that are created as a result of your project, and rewards that are created to complete your project. While brainstorming, you may come up with both types, but the former will be much more effective.

For example, if your project is to make an album, then the result will be a set of songs that you can send to people. Offering the songs as a digital download or CD would probably happen even if you didn't use Kickstarter. However, having a T-Shirt as a reward might attract backers, but is not necessarily something you would make while producing an album.

Sometimes you may need to create additional rewards, but most of the time you will want rewards that are a direct result of your project.

What's in a name?

I bet you already have a name for your project, but do you have a title? Titles are a little different from names. You can name your project anything you like, but it might not make a good title when viewed on the web.

Try to imagine how the title of your project will look when someone posts it on

Facebook or Twitter. Will it make sense? People get hundreds of links each day, so a good title can help them understand what your project is about quickly. Take the title of this project for example: A Kickstarter's Guide to Kickstarter. From this title I know exactly what the project is about. I know that it is being written by someone who has used Kickstarter and the outcome is an e-book.

Good titles capture people's attention and bring them into your project. Titles can be a little mysterious, but they should provide enough information to pique someone's interest. If your title is too generic, people won't be able to tell what you are doing.

For example, "The Green Project" is not a great name because it says nothing about your project. Is the project about saving the earth or building a replica of The Green Monster?

Don't worry if you can't come up with a catchy title just yet. You have until you launch your project to change it. Write down some ideas, test them out, and see which one you like best. Ask your friends or co-workers to see which one piques their interest the most. Naming is hard; so take your time and don't settle on anything too quickly.

Doing Your Homework

Homework

Before you create your project on Kickstarter you will want to do some research. You need to know how much it will cost to execute your project and produce rewards. And you need to know who your audience is going to be. I will examine each of these aspects in more detail, starting with audience since it is often the most overlooked.

The audience

Without an audience, a project will not get funded. You will want to have a good idea about your audience before your project launches. I often find people searching for an audience while their campaign is running. I certainly did this the first time around, and I don't recommend it. If you are lucky enough to already have an online audience, then you probably already know how to reach them. This section is primarily for people who don't have an audience and are trying to build one through a Kickstarter project. For those of you with an audience, you may want to read it anyway. It just might help you appeal to an even larger group of people.

No one cares about you

This is the most important part of the book. If you take away nothing else, try to understand this very difficult lesson about marketing ideas online.

While surfing online looking for advice on marketing, I stumbled upon this video featuring Seth Godin. It's only 1:43 long but it is so powerful.

Seth was interviewed about the explosion of YouTube. "YouTube had five billion videos businesses, how do you put that to work?" Seth cleverly answers the question by explaining that the Internet was not invented to sell ads.

"This is SO important. Ready? No one cares about you! They invented television to sell ads to you. They invented radio to sell ads to you. They invented newspapers to sell ads to you. That's not why they invented YouTube. That's not why they invented the internet."

"The internet doesn't care about you. People don't have to watch channel 7 anymore. They can entertain themselves mindlessly for hours by pressing the StumbleUpon button."

"So, if someone is going to watch a video, they aren't going to watch it because they care about you. They are going to watch it because they care about [themselves]."

The lesson here is that just because you care about the project doesn't mean other people will.

I think one of the biggest false assumptions people make about Kickstarter is that it's going to bring massive amounts of traffic to their idea. Kickstarter is a platform that enables your idea to spread. It does not guarantee that it will.

Don't assume Kickstarter is going to build your audience. You need to do that. You need to do the homework and find all the people who might be interested in your idea. Then if your pitch is good enough, your idea is interesting enough, and your story is compelling enough, you might build something people will care about.

Some People Care About You

Saying that no one cares about you isn't exactly true. It's not that NO ONE cares, it's just that most people aren't going to randomly or instantly fall in love with your idea. Of course, that is what we would like to happen. We want the world to stop and for people to be unable to continue with their day until they have backed our project. But how often does that happen to you?

Most of the time we ignore the hundreds of marketing messages we receive every day. However, every once in a while, we come across something we just can't live without. When that happens, we usually have strong emotional ties and care deeply about it.

In order for your project to be successful, you need to find the people who are going to have a strong emotional connection to it. It's not going to be everyone, and you don't need or want everyone. What you need is a core group or niche of people who will love your idea and bring their friends along.

It Only Takes a Few

One misconception about the way Kickstarter works is that you need hundreds or thousands of people to back a project. This isn't true at all. Just because money is being raised by "the crowd" doesn't mean that the crowd has to be that big. Most projects are funded by a relatively small group of people.

My first project was funded by 170 people. This is a relatively small number considering our goal was $15,000. We didn't get thousands of random people from the Internet to back our project. We just got a few people, mostly family and friends, who cared enough to make our project happen.

Who is Your Audience?

Now it's time to really think about your audience. It will be made up of people from various niche audiences, whose interests are similar to the subject matter of your project. Think about all the different groups of people that might be interested in your project. I do not mean the demographic or any other generic marketing term. I do not mean people who like photography or paintings or any other genre of art. Who is the specific subset of people that are going to LOVE your project? The more specific, the better.

The hard part about defining your audience is that you might not be entirely sure who is going to like your project. That is why you are really going to need to do your homework. You need to have at least one group of people in mind that the project might appeal to.

Ultimately the more niches you can target, the better your chances will be. If you keep targeting the same people they will get tired of hearing about it. People are going to like it or not. Sending it to them more often probably won't change that.

If you are lucky, your project may even appeal to people you had not thought of. However, failing to identify potential groups before your launch will make reaching your goal extremely hard. It's OK to have some unexpected support, but it's risky to leave everything up to chance.

Where is Your Audience?

Now that you have an idea of who your audience is, it is time to start interacting with them. I highly recommend reaching out to your audience well before your project begins. That way you, are part of the community and not some stranger trying to make a fast buck. Of course that's not what you're trying to do, but if the audience doesn't know you, it might come off that way.

If you're passionate about the subject matter, chances are you're already part of an online community. If not, now is the time to start looking. Look for any blog, podcasts, online video shows, forums, or social networks related to your subject matter. Start joining these online communities and try to get a sense of what they're all about. You don't have to contribute right away, but you can if you want.

The important thing is to try to understand what the culture of each community is. When you feel comfortable, start interacting and talking to people about your project. You're not trying to sell it to them, you're just trying to get their feedback. If you want to learn more about how to reach out to online communities effectively, I recommend Gary Vaynerchuk's book Crush It. He is one of the best online marketers and is great at interacting with communities to build an audience.

Do you know anyone off-line that is interested in your subject matter? Ask them what communities they are part of. You can also ask them if they are willing to help promote your idea. Even though Kickstarter is built to spread ideas online, don't be afraid to reach out to people off-line. The combination can be very powerful. Off-line contacts will probably communicate very differently from online contacts. They may send private e-mails and messages to their friends. Those personal forms of communication can be very powerful when trying to recruit support for an idea.

With some projects, talking about your idea early may not be possible. For example, if you're making a product in a very competitive space, you might not feel comfortable about telling people the details of your project. That's okay, but you should still become part of these communities. Maybe you can help in other ways such as giving advice or posting useful links. Do whatever you can to be helpful to others, so when the time comes, they may be willing to help you.

Resonating With Your Audience

You have an audience; you know where to find them, and now you have to figure out how your project is going to connect with them. The more you can align your project with the nuances of your audience the more likely they will like it. You will want your product, your rewards and pitch to resonate with this group of people.

How do you know if this audience will like your project? Try taking a look at the links and posts that they share with each other. This will give you an idea of what they think is important and will be a great place to start. Do any of the topics that are shared have anything in common? Is there something that you can copy or mimic with your own project? Maybe there are very special language, symbols, or gestures that unite this particular group of people. If you can replicate them in an authentic manner, then there's a good chance the community will pick up on it and get behind the idea.

Crossing Chasms

In Crossing the Chasm, Geoffrey A. Moore talks about how new businesses must target a niche to get traction. Once they have established themselves with an initial group of customers, they must work quickly to find other niches. This is because there is a "chasm" between early adopters and the mainstream. The only way to cross is to get a small number of customers from different niches. Once the business has a solid base of customers and is viewed as established, it can be embraced by the mainstream.

Your Kickstarter project is very similar. There is chasm to cross, and the only way to do so is to get a small number of people from different niche audiences to back you.

Once your project has gained enough support to be viewed as "established" it will be much easier for people to back it. Unsuccessful projects struggle to find an audience and gain enough support to cross the chasm.

What Will it Cost?

One aspect of the project that you probably already have in mind is how much money you're going to go for. It's time to dig a little deeper and figure out exactly what it's going to cost to do your project. Your costs will come from the project itself and in fulfilling rewards. You will want to have a good idea about how much money you will need for each of these areas. They will play an important role during the next phase when you must set your funding amount.

For the product, look up different prices related to the item you are trying to produce. For example, if you are making a book, look online at all of the different printing options. What is the cost of a hardcover? What is the cost of a softcover? How much does it cost to ship the item? How many do you need to produce before you get a discount? What supplies or materials do you need to complete the project? Do you need specialized instruments or tools? Make a list of everything that you will need and how much it will cost. You will need to come back to this list later.

For rewards, make sure you research shipping costs as well as production costs. If one of your rewards is going to be a T-shirt, then you will need to know how much it costs to make and ship the item. Often people don't factor in the cost of rewards into their funding and then are left without enough money to complete their project.

One example of someone who might not have put enough time into researching

her costs is Paula Patterson. According to a *New York Times article*, On Kickstarter, Designers' Dreams Materialize, her V-luxe iPad entertainment accessory ended up costing a lot more time and money than she originally thought.

You may already have an idea of what your project is going to cost in total. However, now is the time to refine that estimate.

Profit margin

When someone backs your project and selects a reward, there is a cost associated with producing that item. The difference between what it costs you to produce the reward, and the amount of money a backer pledges, is the profit margin. Kickstarter projects aren't really about making a "profit," but it's one of the most important metrics in business and can help you structure your project effectively.

Lets say you are offering a DVD and DVDs cost about $5 to produce. It also costs a dollar to ship the DVD to your backers. That means the total cost to produce the DVD is about $6. If you sold a DVD for $10, and it costs you $6 to produce then you are making $4 of profit. This profit is going to be used to complete the rest of your project, and having a poor profit margin can hurt your ability to complete it.

If the example project got 100 backers who chose the DVD, then one might think the project creator has received $1000. However, when the cost to produce the DVDs is removed, the creator only made $400 in profit. You need to make sure the profit margin is great enough to honor the reward system and still cover the project's cost. I will get into how to price rewards later, but right now, you need to know what it will cost you to produce all the items you want to make.

Not every Kickstarter venture is launched with the intent of making money. However, if you want to launch a project as a business, having a healthy profit margin is important.

"'If I was being realistic, we probably needed $10,000 to $15,000 to get started, and these things should cost at least $750,' she added. 'Below $750 is a losing enterprise.'"

- Paula Patterson On Kickstarter, Designers' Dreams Materialize, NY Times

Fixed and Varible Costs

When creating your budget, you need to account for both the fixed cost and variable costs.

Fixed costs - The costs that will not change as the number of backers increases. This could be the cost of supplies, travel, or any other expense related to the creation of your project.

Variable costs - The cost that will change depending on the number of backers you receive. These costs can go up or down, but the important thing is that they change. For example, if you're making a book the more backers you receive, the more shipping costs you have. However, it will be cheaper to produce the book since many publishers give discounts for larger orders.

Setting Your Goals

Make or Break Decisions

Probably the three most difficult questions of any Kickstarter project are how much, how long, and how to price rewards. This section is all about how to approach these crucial decisions.

While researching this book I came across a post call Kickstartup by Craig Mod. It provides some detailed analyses and great insights on these very tough questions. I highly recommend checking it out, as it was mentioned by most of my interviewees as an important reference.

How Much?

Picking your funding amount is difficult, because if you go for too much, you risk losing it all. With Kickstarter's all or nothing model, the biggest risk you take is setting your funding goal too high.

I will look at why it is so difficult to get large amounts of money from Kickstarter and why you might be better off going for a smaller amount. I know what you are thinking.

What about those people who make tens of thousands of dollars for their projects? A lot of those are outliers. I want to talk about what a typical project can expect.

Running the numbers

Why is it so hard to get a large project funded? Because of the sheer number of people who need to visit the project page. A project can be funded by a relatively small number of backers, but those backers come from a large group of people who have looked at the project, and most have not contributed.

According to Kickstarter, the average pledge is $70. Lets say your goal is $10,000. To raise this much money you will need between 130 to 150 backers. I found the number of backers is often lower, meaning people often pledge more than $70, but it's a good place to start.

Based on my research, Kickstarter has about a 10% conversion rate. This means if you send the project to 100 people, 10 will back it. I'll explain in the section "Launching

Your Project" how I calculated this number. In the example above, the project needed

150 people to be funded. Assuming a 10% conversion rate, the project will need to be seen by 1500 people. Some of the views could be repeats, but it still needs to be seen by more than a thousand individuals.

A project that needs $40,000 will have to be viewed 5000+ times. Now you can start to see where this gets difficult. Unless you already have an audience or a large network, it is going to be very hard to reach that many people. If you think of everyone you know and could possibly reach out to, it's probably a few hundred people. So the only way to get 1500 views is for your contacts to share your project with their contacts.

Focus on What You Need

It's time to focus on your budget and really look at what you need to make the project work, because setting your goals too high might actually hurt you. It takes a lot of work to get a project funded and you should be realistic about what your needs are.

This was one mistake my co-producer and I made during my own campaign that almost cost us the project. John and I debated whether we should go for $20,000 or $15,000. Obviously, when making a movie you want as much money as possible. We went back and forth but ultimately decided on $15,000. The thinking was that we would hope for higher amount and have the lower amount as a safety net. I am so glad we made that decision, because in all honesty, I don't think there was any way we would have made it to $20,000. It turned out $15,000 was just in our reach.

Look at all of your research and try to determine what is the minimum amount that you need to do your project. You may have a bigger vision for your project, but try to keep it small at first. The goal should be to get funded. If you do a really great job and get overfunded, then you might be able to do your project as envisioned. However, if you don't get funded, you might not be able to do anything.

Should you undershoot your goal? No. Be honest about how much your project is going to cost. If you need to raise $50,000 minimum to do your project, then that's your goal, not $35,000. Do the work and figure out exactly what you will need to complete your project and its reward obligations.

Reasonable goals

So what are some reasonable expectations for funding amounts?

- For a single person with a limited or no built-in audience, $5000 or less is manageable, $5000 to $10,000 will be hard but doable, $10,000+ will be very hard.

- For projects with more than one creator and a limited or no built-in audience, each creator can probably bring in $7000, assuming their networks do not overlap too much.

- For projects with established audiences it really depends on the size of your audience. Nataly Dawn raised $104,788 from 2315 backers, but one look at her Youtube channel shows over 88,000 subscribers. Videos from her group Pomplamoose get over a million views. The majority of her backers are people who have been following her for awhile.

You are free to set your funding goal to whatever you want. Just keep in mind how many people you will need to look at your project to get it funded. Even the "most funded" projects on Kickstarter have relatively small goals compared to what they were able to raise.

Why be Reasonable?

Of course you don't necessarily have to play it safe. Craig Mod provides an interesting counterpoint to the "be reasonable" argument.

> **"Our biggest mistake was that we set our financial goal too low. It's inevitable that a Kickstarter project becomes less exciting and loses its 'gambling' element when the financial goal is met and there's still time on the clock (just look at our funding graphs above for empirical evidence!). An ideal situation for any Kickstarter project is to define a financial goal that is high enough to just be met within the allotted time."**
> *- Craig Mod, Kickstartup*

Perhaps for Craig's project, the goal was set too low, and it might have been able to get more backers.

However, I just want to point out what I think is the key sentence in his entire post.

> **"We took advantage of the vast contact lists we had built up while working in the design and art worlds over the past six years."**
> *- Craig Mod, Kickstartup*

To me, this demonstrates that Craig had a large existing audience before launching the Kickstarter project and therefore could have gone for more money.

Personally, I think it is better to get funded at a lower level than to be too ambitious and not get anything. Of course, the risk is yours. I reiterate: unless you have a relatively large existing audience, it is going to be very hard to generate $10,000 or more.

How Long?

One of the emotionally difficult decisions you will have to make is how long to run your campaign. As soon as you press go, the clock starts ticking, and it doesn't stop or wait for you to figure things out. This can bring a lot of stress because your entire project is at stake.

However, the clock can also be a powerful ally. It forces people to choose whether they're going to help you or not, and it gets the word out quickly. If everything goes well, the clock can rally your supporters and make your project a success.

Setting the length of your Kickstarter campaign is about sustaining momentum and meeting production deadlines. The maximum campaign length is 60 days, but as you will see, you may want to run a shorter campaign.

Momentum

Projects that can sustain momentum over time will do well. Most campaigns will see a lot of activity at the beginning and the end, with a lull in the middle. Setting the time limit on the project is really about guessing how much momentum you can sustain during your project.

This is very hard to judge, and I have no real way of predicting this. Some projects that I think are going to do well, don't make it, or only finish at the last minute. Other projects that I'm unsure about get funded right away. It is hard to say exactly where momentum comes from, but you should be prepared to deal with it.

In his blog Kickstartup, Craig Mod talks about planning media coverages to avoid "dead zones" in momentum. You can see from all the wonderful data he provides that there were several days in the middle of the project where pledging dropped off. Try to have a strategy for dealing with a drop in momentum, but be aware it's part of the process.

30 days or less

According to Kickstarter's Kickstart School: Setting Your Goal page, statistically the most successful projects run for 30 days or less. Since they have data on projects, I would say this is a good number to go by.

During my interview with Dan Provost, co-creator of the iPhone tripod mount Glif, he explained why shorter campaigns are better.

"Anything longer than 30 days was kind of unnecessarily long. It's either going to hit or it's not. And if it doesn't, then you are kind of dragging it out."

I think this is a great way of looking at the timing. If people like your idea, they will like it right away. A longer campaign won't necessarily make the idea any more attractive. He also makes the point that the attention span for things on the Internet is usually less than 30 days.

Managing Deadlines

Another factor to consider is your own personal deadlines. In both of my Kickstarter projects the timing and length of my campaign was set by outside factors. I wanted to hit deadlines and timing windows which forced me launch at times that might not have been optimal.

You may have some timing windows that you are trying to hit. Meeting these timing windows can be tricky, because you run the risk of not putting enough work into your campaign before it launches.

The most important factor here is the size of your project and how much you're going for. If you have a tight timing window and a smaller size project, then you might need to launch before you have worked everything out. If you're going for a large amount and have a big project, then it will pay off to wait until you have everything ready to launch a campaign. Trying to launch before you are ready in order to hit an arbitrary deadline might hurt you. If I had to do it over again, I would've spent several months preparing for my first Kickstarter project instead of rushing to get it out the door.

Pricing Rewards

The Creating Rewards page of the Kickstarter school informs you that the most common pledge is $25 and the average pledge is $70. You do not have to have these price points, but it might be a good idea to create tiers at or around these price points. Craig Mod provides further insight with his analysis of the top projects during March, 2010. He found that the highest grossing reward amounts were $25, $50, $100, $250 and $500. Craig concludes that people don't mind paying $50 or higher for projects they love.

Going for the Big Bucks

I see a lot of rewards in the thousand dollar range on Kickstarter. Sometimes projects even skip the most lucrative pledging tiers altogether, going from $20 to $200 to $1000. To me this is another example of people misunderstanding how Kickstarter works. The idea of crowd-sourced funding is that a lot of people will pledge smaller amounts of money. Pricing rewards in the thousands of dollars contradicts this idea. It is very hard to get people to spend large amounts of money on a perfect stranger.

In my experience, pledges of a $1000 or more came from people who knew me BEFORE I ran the campaign, not people who found me online. They are close family and friends who wanted to support our work. If someone is going to pledge in the thousands, you probably already know them. They already believe in your project, and you may have an inkling they will pledge at that level. You could have the coolest rewards in the world, but it probably won't convince people who don't know you to back at that level. Then again, if you are catering to an audience that regularly pays $1000+ for products, it just might work.

The Allure of a Large Backer

While large backers definitely give your project a boost, they also take away from the size of your new audience. One of the biggest benefits to Kickstarter is that it allows you to talk to more people. Every time you post an update, you get into the inbox of people who want to hear from you. Large backers are, in a way, a double-edged sword. They help your project, but hurt your reach.

Let's say you launch a project for $3000. You get six backers and raise $400. Then a BIG backer pledges $2000 and almost completes your project. Now you only have a handful of people you can talk to. One of the best things to come out of my first project was the 170 people I can now talk to directly. Next time I want to launch a creative project I have a small group of people that I can share the idea with first.

Quantity OF Quality

When creating rewards the goal should be to have an adequate quantity of quality backers. You want to design the rewards so that most people will pledge right in the middle of your reward levels. You want some high backers and some low backers with most falling in the middle. Having a good spread of rewards, especially in the $25 to $250 range, will really help get a solid group of backers.

Pricing Theory

The psychology of pricing is very difficult and complex. This book is too short to really get into it, but here are some things to think about. If you would like an in-depth look at pricing theory, I recommend Smart Pricing by Z. John Zhang

People enjoy a purchase more if they pay more for it. This is counter-intuitive. A common misconception is that people are very price sensitive, and always look for the best possible price. That might be true for food or gas, but most people coming to Kickstarter want to connect with other people. Stay away from really high reward levels, but don't undervalue your rewards either.

If a higher priced reward is not significantly better, then why pay more? The tricky part about creating rewards is increasing value to match the increase in price. For example, if you are making an album you could offer a digital download and a CD as rewards. But, how much more valuable is a CD vs the digital download? I don't mean monetary value but sentimental value. If the download is $10 and the CD is $25 is there enough of a difference that I would purchase the higher priced reward? For me, no. In fact I might pay you $15 extra NOT to make a CD. What's the point? It wastes resources and gets scratched. However, if your CD is personally burned, and has an extra track, and sold for $50, then it might be a compelling enough reward.

The Paradox of Choice

We love choice. In any given year every single film on Netflix is watched at least once.

The Long Tail is an economic theory and excellent book, which explains why this happens. It states that due to the infinite shelf space of online retailers, people will now have almost limitless choices as to what they consume. We are living in a world where people can find exactly what they're looking for and are willing to pay unbelievably high prices to get those special unique items.

At the same time, we hate choice. Having too many choices when we don't have a lot of time, can be overwhelming and confusing. Limitless choice works when people have the time and energy to pay attention and look for the very best. When they don't, people want quick and easy choices.

The Coffee Joulies project is one of the top-funded design projects on Kickstarter, and it has only three backing levels. It's simple, and people visiting the page do not have to think much about what level they are going to choose.

Then again, the Womanthology; Massive All Female Comic Anthology! project was incredibly successful with a very complex system of rewards and almost 50 different backing levels. They even had unlockable rewards that, like in video games, became available when a certain goal was reached. This, however, was probably planned out ahead of time, and a lot of work went into putting them all together.

When creating your rewards, it is probably to best make ones that have meaningful value. If you are having trouble coming up with a $5 reward, then maybe you don't need one. Having too many rewards ultimately clutters up your page and makes it difficult for people to decide. However, you may want to have a lot of different rewards. Either way, make it a conscious decision. Creating rewards just to fill price points probably won't be meaningful enough for backers.

Crafting Your Pitch

The Pitch

Each project page on Kickstarter is essentially a pitch for an idea, your idea. When people come to Kickstarter they are coming to be pitched. They aren't actively thinking this of course, but they want to hear about you and your project. The pitch can make or break a project, so having a good one is important.

A Kickstarter pitch usually consists of an image, video, and written copy. While most people choose to do a video it is not required. However, the Kickstarter School highly recommends that you do a video. It is a great way for people who don't know you to learn about you and your idea.

This section examines how to use the video and copy to pitch your idea and get backers. There are several questions people will have about your project that they will want answered. Answering those questions can, in some circumstances, double your chances of a viewer becoming a backer. This section is not about how to make your video or what to write about. That is beyond the scope of this book.

What makes a good pitch?

Good pitches have three essential elements: narrative, credibility, and clarity. You don't need to have all three in your pitch, but a successful project does at least one of them very well.

Narrative - Your personal story and the story behind your idea. If you can explain why you are excited about the project and what led you to create it, then people will have a much easier time connecting with you. Credibility - This is one aspect of the pitch that people often miss. You want to show people that you are the right person to do this project. You achieve this by showing prototypes of your product or samples of your art. The more previous experience you can demonstrate, the more people will trust you.

Clarity - Keep it simple. Don't make people guess what your project is or what the result is going to be. The easier it is for people to understand your project, the easier it is for them make a decision about whether to back you.

Narrative

The sequence of events that lead to your Kickstarter project is the narrative. It is the story of how this project came into existence, and a statement of why you are trying to raise funds. As you build your narrative there are four questions potential backers want you to answer.

Who are you? - This can be as simple as your name. People who don't know you will be viewing this project, so introduce yourself.

What are you doing? - Explain what your project is about and what the result is going to be. You can also talk about how you arrived at this project and the history behind it.

Why is it important? - Are you passionate about this idea? Tell us why. Explain to us why the project is so cool. Passion draws people in, even if they don't love the subject matter as much as you.

What is the money for? - When answering this question you can be very specific or general, it's really up to you. "I'm building a prototype" or "I'm using the money to get the book printed" are both acceptable explanations of what the money is for. Saying nothing is also an option, but probably not a good idea for larger projects.

Crafting a Story

You might be thinking: I don't have a good story. Yes you do. Your project must have come from somewhere. Tell us about how you got started and why you love the idea. It doesn't have to be complicated or in-depth, it just has to be you. The more personal and authentic the better. If your project is about bottle caps, tell us how you got started collecting and why they are so awesome. Make us love your subject matter as much as you do.

Credibility

If there is one thing people should do to make their projects better, it would be to demonstrate more credibility. I really think this is the missing ingredient in a lot of Kickstarter campaigns. The more credibility you show, the better. I don't think you can have enough of it.

In the Kickstarter world this could mean a couple different things. If you are launching a product, then having a working prototype is very important. If you are doing a more artistic project, then show your work in the video and on the page. If you are making an album, then let us hear an example of your music.

According to the folks at Eureka Ranch, whose innovations appear in many household

products, you double the odds of a sale when you communicate real "reason to believe." The simplest way to do this, is to tell the truth and show your work.

Ideas Are Easy

At the end of a video for The Daily: Business Gary Vaynerchuk makes an excellent point about execution.

> **"Nobody is investing in ideas...execution is the game. I'm not interested in investing in your idea, everyone has one. Show me if you can execute it, show me a tangible product. That gets people like us excited."**

Ideas are easy. The execution is hard. People want to see that you can carry out what you say. This is why demonstrating your credibility is so important.

If you don't have a solid working prototype or examples of your work, then maybe you aren't ready for Kickstarter yet. That's OK. Launching a creative project is hard. Don't rush it because you want to do it right now. Take the idea as far as you can before you launch on Kickstarter. It will make the whole process so much easier.

Clarity

Your pitch should be short and to the point. People are busy and don't have time to watch a long video or read a lot of text.

Burying the lead

> **"In journalism, the failure to mention the most interesting or attention grabbing elements of a story in the first paragraph is sometimes called 'burying the lead.'"**
>
> *- Lead paragraph, Wikipedia*

This is also true for your pitch. Make sure you open with your most interesting elements. You want people to be interested in your project from the start.

Refine, Refine Refine

In my interviews with Peter and Dan they both stressed the need to constantly refine your pitch until you get at the very core of your idea.

> **"Boil it down, more concise, more instant. [With] the attention span of a citizen in today's world, if you get two minutes that's amazing."**
> *- Peter Dering*

> **"We put a lot of thought into the project page and wanted it to be carefully crafted to showed that we cared... You want to make that story as crystal clear as possible."**
> *- Dan Provost*

The Ask

A small detail of the pitch, which is often overlooked, are the specific words you use to ask for support. There are many different ways to ask people to back your project, and I think some are more effective that others. I don't have any data to back up this claim, but for me the way you ask can really affect people's decision-making. When done right, it can give people confidence about backing your project.

If you want to see how a pro does it, watch this video with Gary Vaynerchuk, as he asks you to pre-order and support his then, new book, Crush It. The ask comes 1:27 into the video, but make sure you look at the whole thing, so you can see how he builds to it. It's so subtle you almost miss it. He is intentional about asking for your support but very authentic.

Asking for support is tricky, because you don't want to be too commercial, and you don't want to beg either. While the ask is not one of the four key pitch elements, when done effectively, it can actually persuade people to back your project.

Your Project is Not Charity

Is your project a charity? No? Then why are you asking for donations? Charities are really important, but your project isn't be one of them. A lot of people ask for donations in their pitches. To me the word "donation" is closely linked to charities and implies that the value exchanged is primarily for social good. Kickstarter is about exchanging value and giving your backers something in return. In fact Kickstarter clearly says no charities on it's project guidelines page.

> **"This is a place for creative people. It's not a place for charity."**
> *- Perry Chen Rocketboom interview*

How to Ask

There are many ways to ask for someone for support on Kickstarter. Here are a few ways I might ask.

"I hope you back my project."

"With your support..."

"You will be pre-ordering this item."

"Backing this project will help bring it to market."

"If you like the project, then please back it."

The Video

"80% of Kickstarter projects at this point launch with videos. We are very much a video-driven site. People land on the page, they hit play, they want to see what's there."
- Yancey Strickler Creative Mornings June 2011

The project video is an important part of the pitch. It allows people to get to know you and connect with your subject matter. There are a ton of things that you can do with your video. You can shoot it cinematically or just use a web camera. You can be funny or serious. It really doesn't matter, as long as it is a true reflection of you.

Good Audio

One of my pet peeves are videos that don't have good audio. If I can't hear you, then I can't connect with you. If you are going through all this trouble to make a video, then don't ruin it with bad audio. Find someone who can lend you some good equipment or buy a decent microphone. Either way, make the extra effort so that your video will have the maximum effect.

How Fancy Should it Be?

I think this has to do with how much money you are trying to raise. In my mind, the more money you are trying to raise, the more professional your video should be. This builds your credibility and helps people see that you can articulate your vision.

Some Examples

Here are some examples of people who pitch their project exceptionally well. As you will see, the videos can be basic or professionally done.

Save Blue Like Jazz (Narrative)

In the video to save the movie Blue Like Jazz, Zack and Jonathan do a great job of explaining all the events leading to their campaign. They answer all the important questions and rally the fans to make the movie happen.

SAVE Blue Like Jazz! (the movie) by Steve Taylor —
Kickstarter

Capture clip (Credibility)

Just one look at this video, and you can tell how much he loves his idea and how much work went into creating it. He has a prototype that he has been working on for over a year. You can see he just needs a little help to bring it to life. You can't help but cheer for him as he has clearly spent a long time on this project.

Capture Camera Clip System by Peter Dering —
Kickstarter

The Manual (Clarity)

The video for The Manual, a magazine about design, is a perfect example of a clear pitch. It is short and to the point. You understand what the project is and what the end result will be.

The Manual by Andy McMillan — Kickstarter

The Night Parade of One Hundred Demons (The Ask)

This simple webcam pitch NAILS it. I was blown away by this guy's pitch and ended up backing him. He shows passion and excitement for his project. My favorite part? The Ask: "I'm asking for your patronage to help me make this book." He didn't ask for donations or support. He asked for your patronage, perfect! Just look at how much money he raised.

The Night Parade of One Hundred Demons by Matthew Meyer — Kickstarter

Launching Your Project

Two Types of Launches

There's the soft launch and the actual launch.

The soft launch is everything that you do before the Kickstarter project goes live. This involves building awareness and gaining support for an idea before you are ready to start.

The actual launch is when you finally push the button on Kickstarter and your project is live. Once your project is launched you will use the contacts built up during the soft launch to help promote the project.

Soft Launch

The soft launch is a concept I came across while researching A Kickstarter's Guide. In his post 15 steps for a successful Kickstarter Project Gary M. Sarli talks about the idea of a soft launch.

"(7) Do a soft launch for the project on your website and via social media at least 30 days before you start the actual Kickstarter project. You want to get the word out and get people interested and talking before you start the fundraising drive itself. At this stage, you'll need to be able to tell people firm dates for the start and end of the Kickstarter drive, reward levels for backers, and so forth; use your own website as the central location for this because you won't have a Kickstarter page to send people to until later."

"Go to any message boards you frequent to post about the project (but don't be spammy — if you don't regularly post somewhere, don't announce in that forum). Include links to the project in your message board profile and signature."

"There are plenty of other websites and blogs that might be interested, so don't be shy about getting in touch with them to tell them about the project (perhaps as a formal press release). For example, if doing a roleplaying game project, you might submit a short press release to ENWorld to see if they'll include it in their news feed for the day."

"Get all your friends and colleagues on board; the more voices you can get talking about the project, the better your odds will be."

Doing a soft launch is something I have not been very good at. For both, Identifying Nelson, and A Kickstarter's Guide, I did not spend enough time reaching out to people before they launched. This meant that during my campaigns, I was forced to spend a lot of time looking for an audience, instead of promoting the project. Not only is this stressful, but finding the right audience can take a long time. Trying to do it during a campaign is very challenging.

Reach Out

By now you should have found where your audience communicates and become part of that community. Then you should start talking with them about the project and when it will go live. Share with them your idea and let them know you are thinking of running it as Kickstarter campaign. They may like it or they may hate it. Either way, take it with a grain of salt. I've had plenty of people love my ideas and then never back my projects. Conversely people might not understand what you are trying to do until it is live. The point is to start the conversation as early as possible.

Actual Launch

Once you have reached out to your communities, it is time to push the button and go for it!

At this point your nerves will probably start to "kick in" and you will be wondering if you got everything right. There is only one way to find out. Launch.

> **"Real artists ship."**
> *- Steve Jobs*

Best Time to Launch

I'm not sure if it matters. Just know that the campaign ends at the same time that you press the button. So, if you push it at 2 a.m., your campaign ends at 2 a.m.

I realized that in the future I am going to want my campaign to end at night. This is because I had difficulty falling asleep knowing my campaign was ending in the morning. The project was already funded, but I was so excited to see the result that I just couldn't fall asleep. Next time, I will be sure to start my project at night so it will finish before I go to bed.

Find the Fans

When you start your campaign, you will want to be on the lookout for your fans. They are the people who are going to go out of their way to make your project successful. They will help spread the word by writing on your behalf. They will get their friends and family to back the project. They will help you "cross the chasm."

During my first campaign, my friend Caroline was my biggest fan. She went out of her way to email friends, get her family on board, and anything else she could think of. Without her, I'm pretty sure my project would not have succeeded. Caroline, if you are reading this, thank you!

How does it spread?

Once the project has launched, pay attention to where people are talking about it.

During my first campaign, Facebook was the most effective marketing tool. During my second, it was Twitter and Kickstarter.com. If you have been doing your homework, you should have an idea of where your audience hangs out. Concentrate on the sites and methods that gain the most traction. Don't try to promote your project on every medium because you think that's what you need to do. If your audience isn't on Twitter, then don't post as often. Posting on networks that aren't part of your audience annoys people, makes Kickstarter look bad, and won't get your project funded.

Project Updates

These are a very useful both during and after the campaign. During the campaign, you can post about its progress. It's a great way to keep your backers involved and enlist their additional support. You can thank them, and ask them to share the project with their networks.

After the campaign is over, you can keep in touch with them about the project and let them know the status of their rewards.

Project updates are great. Use them! I don't think I used them enough. We didn't write our first update until halfway through the campaign. You don't need to write updates if you don't have anything to say, but you want to engage the people who backed you. Even if its just to say thank you. In fact, you can't say thank you often enough.

Tracking Your Progress

Now that your campaign is underway, how do you know if it's going well or not? Here are some of the things I do.

The Short link

Every Kickstarter project page has a short link. This is smaller version of its web address. It can be found on your main project page, below the picture/video for

your project. You will see it to the right of the "<>
EMBED" button.

When you are promoting your project, you will want to
use the short link as often as possible. Not only is it
easier to share, but it can be used to calculate some
important metrics about your project.

The only downside is that it doesn't include
kickstarter.com in the address. Some people might be
hesitant to click on the short link, because they don't
know where it is taking them. However, if you are the
one sharing it, and they trust you, then you should have
no problem.

Conversion Rate

The conversion rate can be a powerful tool in
determining the reach of your campaign and how much
work you still have to do. This works best if you have
been using your project short link during the whole
campaign. WARNING: This will require a little math, but
nothing too complicated.

First, find the total number of clicks the project is getting, by adding a + sign to the end of the short link.

Like this: http://kck.st/ghhocJoTE+

This will take you to an info page for bitly.com, which creates and hosts all of Kickstarter's short links. Towards the top of the page, there are two numbers, one in bold, which represent the number of clicks the link is getting. You will want to use the number NOT in bold This can be found next to the words: "All clicks on the aggregate bitly link"

Next you will need the number of people backing your project from the Kickstarter project page. Divide the number of backers by the total number of clicks your short link has received. This will be the conversation rate. For example, if a project has 14 backers and 180 clicks then the conversion rate is 7%.

14 Backers / 180 Clicks = 7% Conversion rate

Average Pledge Amount

The next important metric is the average amount pledged. This will help you figure out, on average, what each person is giving to the project. Later it will help you figure out how many backers you still need.

Take the amount pledged towards your project so far, and divide that by the number of backers. If your project has raised $245 from 14 backers, then the average pledge is $17.50

$245 Pledged / 14 Backers = $17.50 per backer

Remaining Views and Backers

Next you want to calculate the remaining views in order to get enough backers to meet your minimum funding goal.

Divide the remaining pledge amount by the average pledge amount. If your goal is $900, and you have raised $245, then you still need $655. Take this remaining amount, and divide that by the average pledge amount. So, if the average pledge amount is $17.50, then you need 38 more backers to finish the project. (I rounded up, since you don't want to underestimate the number of backers you need.)

$900 Goal - $245 Pledged = $655 Remaining

$655 Remaining / $17.50 Avg. Pledge = 38 Backers

Once you know how many backers you still need, you can use the conversion rate to figure out how many views you need to get those backers.

Take the number of people you still need, and multiply it by the conversion rate. In this example, there are 38 backers remaining and a 7% conversion rate. This means the project will need close to 542 clicks to get the project funded.

38 Backers Remaining * 7% Conversion Rate = 542 Clicks

Fuzzy Math

These numbers are not exact, of course. They depend on a number of factors. As your project evolves, the numbers will change, so you can recalculate them as often as you need. These are just indicators of how your campaign is going. Your might post the link somewhere and get 500 more clicks, but if it's the wrong 500 people, then you will not meet your goal. These metrics will give you valuable feedback, but they are not predictive of the outcome.

However, I have found these numbers to be very relevant and helpful. The example above uses numbers taken from my campaign. If you did all the math, then you may have realized 54 backers were needed to get the project funded. The actual number, ended up being 56 backers. Not bad at all.

The Tipping Point

One of the most fascinating aspects of Kickstarter is the project's "tipping point," the point at which a project has enough momentum that it will most likely be completed. In Yancey Strickler's Creative Mornings presentation, he explains how a project that reaches 30% funding has a 90% chance of being successfully completed.

I learned of the 30% tipping point during my campaign. At the time I found it hard to believe. I couldn't imagine how a project with 70% of its funding goal left had such a good chance of making it. Even when the project passed its tipping point, I was still skeptical. But to my amazement we made it.

Initially, I thought the 30% tipping point had to do with having a critical mass of backers. Once a project got enough backers to fund 30%, then that group would bring in the rest of the backers. It turns out that the number of backers it takes to reach 30% is quite low. During my campaign it was only 16 people. Each person would have had to bring in three to four more people. While this might have happened, I think critical mass isn't the only factor in play.

More recently, I began to think that there could be a psychological barrier before a project is 30% funded. When viewing the little green progress bar, a project with less than 30% funding looks like it won't make it. Once that barrier is broken, people are more likely to jump on board. One thing that is clear about Kickstarter. People like to support projects that are going to make it. Maybe there is something about the 30% mark that subconsciously signals eventual success.

We may never know why 30% is such an important number, but it almost doesn't matter. What matters is getting to that mark as quickly as possible. Try your hardest to get to 30%. Then you can ease off a bit until you need to do a big push at the end.

Conclusion

Idea & Story

These are the two fundamental building blocks of any Kickstarter project. A great project embodies a remarkable idea or tells a compelling story. The very best projects use both idea and story to build an audience and attract backers.

Unlike the other concepts in this book, these two principles affect all aspects of your endeavor. They can be embedded in everything, from what you are producing, to the way that you run your campaign. Using them well is extremely hard, but the payoff can be incredibly high.

Capturing an Idea

Ideas are powerful. They are like viruses, spreading form person to person. When your project embodies a remarkable idea, it too will spread and this can serve as your marketing.

There are some projects on Kickstarter that have been funded because they represent an idea so contagious that people can't help but talk about them. Building a stature of Robocop in downtown Detroit is one such idea. These type of projects are rare, but you can use this principle to make your project more interesting.

When Dan Provost & Tom Gerhardt ran their second Kickstarter project, they tried something different with their pricing. During their first project The Glif, they set the price of their product at $25. For their second project, a wide grip stylus for tablets, they did not set a price. They said the item would retail for $25, but people were able to pledge whatever they wanted. The catch was that there were only 3000 slots to raise $50,000. If everyone pledged $1, then no one would get the reward. By using a creative pricing model, they captured an idea that got people talking.

Everyone is making a film, album, art project, comic book, novel, etc., so you should want to create a project that represents an idea worth talking about.

Telling a Great Story

Story is the other building block you have to play with. Telling your story in a compelling manner can make an ordinary project shine. Storytelling isn't just the narrative of how your project came into existence. It is about entertaining people and connecting with them on an emotional level. It's more than your video, although that may be the primary medium. It is the way you convey the story that reveals the essence of your project.

Zach Williams and The Bellow used storytelling as a critical element in their project to record an album. Recording an album is not a new, creative, or even that interesting of an idea, but the way they talked about it was. In the video Zach talks about how eight strangers from the South found each other in New York City and formed the band. He talks about what the music means to them and why it is so important. Through their video you understand that, for them, this is about much more than just recording an album.

As you build your project, think about the elements that will make your story more compelling, and how you want to express them. There might even be things you can do that will enhance the story when the project launches. Give it some real thought, because a great story can turn an ordinary idea into something magical.

Worst Case Scenario

You've read this guide, you've researched other projects, you've found an audience, and you've created a compelling pitch, but your project didn't make it. You did everything you could to drum up support, but it still wasn't enough. That's okay. Maybe your idea wasn't ready. Maybe you didn't explain yourself clearly enough. You aren't necessarily going to get it right the first time. Before I came to Kickstarter I launched many other projects, most of which failed. It was learning from those failures that ultimately helped me be successful.

One of the best aspects about Kickstarter is that you risk very little when launching a project. So even if it fails, it's not really that bad. You will probably be disappointed, but at least you didn't spend a lot of time and money creating something, only to find it's not what people want. You will have learned about yourself and have a better idea how to launch a project. All of that experience will be valuable the next time around.

What's left?

Courage.

Courage to do something meaningful. Courage to silence that voice in your head that makes you doubt yourself. Courage to launch your project into the world.

Overcoming our fears is never easy, but its part of the process. In a world filled with so much uncertainty, we need people who will stand up and make a difference. You may think your project isn't that important, but you never know who you will inspire. Many of the people I talked with, said how the success of other projects got them to launch their own. So go out there and make something happen.

CPSIA information can be obtained at www.ICGtesting.com
Printed in the USA
LVOW07s0201271014

410579LV00001B/31/P